LOOKING BACK AT CLASSIC TANKERS
by
Andrew Wiltshire

The name **Cerinthus** was that of a Christian heretic of the first century, and for 22 years was the name carried by this steam tanker in the fleet of Hadley Shipping Co Ltd. The **Cerinthus** was an example of a Shell Tankers H class 18000dwt design being completed on 9 November 1954. She was built by Harland and Wolff at Belfast and was 12174grt and 19180dwt. Her overall length was 555 feet and her breadth was 69 feet. The **Cerinthus** was a steam ship with Harland & Wolff turbines of 8250shp which gave her an average speed of 14 knots. In the Hadley fleet she joined the motor tanker **Corato** of 1952 which was on charter to BP. The **Cerinthus** is seen arriving at Cardiff for drydocking on 20 May 1974. Just over two years later she was broken up at Faslane in Scotland. She arrived there on 23 July 1976 and was moored alongside the British tanker **El Lobo** (see page 53).

(John Wiltshire)

Introduction

A tanker is a vessel built to transport liquids in bulk. For centuries man has carried a variety of liquids including oil by sea, but it was not until 1886 that a vessel built especially to carry oil in bulk was constructed. Designs evolved and in 1908 far greater hull strength was achieved with the introduction of longitudinal framing. This became known as the Isherwood system, pantented in 1906 and first used in the **Paul Paix** in August 1908. Based on the Isherwood system of frames, the cargo space of a tanker is divided into separate tanks. This reduces the overall free surface of the cargo and therefore improves stability at sea. It also enables oils of various grades to be carried in the various tanks. The size of tankers steadily increased, but it was in the early 1950s that a dramatic increase in size took place. A deadweight tonnage of around 45,000 was at this time considered to be very large. By 1959 this had exceeded 100,000dwt and by 1968 the **Universe Ireland** was built with a dwt of 312,000.

For decades tanker design was very conventional, with the bridge and officer accommodation amidships and the machinery space and remaining accommodation situated aft. This started to change in the 1950s when a number of owners specified new tankers with the bridge and all accommodation situated aft. Motor tankers first appeared in the 1920s, but steam propulsion remained very popular for tankers well into the 1960s. Very large tankers continued to use steam propulsion long after it had become uneconomical in other types of ship. Tankers of course need large quantities of steam for tank heating and also for some auxiliaries like winches where electric motors cannot be used for safety reasons. Most oils transported by ship are mineral based oils in crude or refined forms. Over the years though, tankers have been built to carry vegetable oils as well as liquid gases in pressurised tanks and bulk chemicals. All these require special design considerations.

This book sets out to portray the many types of tanker to be found sailing worldwide in the years after World War 2, most of which had disappeared by the 1980s. Their careers and ultimate fates are often very diverse, and highlight the great variety that could be found sailing under different owners and flags.

Acknowledgements

Once again a thank you goes out to the many photographers who have made their work available to me for use in this book. Without their kind cooperation this book would not have been possible. Many thanks to my father John Wiltshire who has once again kept me supplied with material from which to make my selections. A very big thank you must go to my good friend Kevin Blair who has helped enormously in researching and checking data for me. Also many thanks to another good friend Nigel Jones, for his extensive research on a number of the vessels featured in this book. Paul Boot has given the book an extra special feel by making available images from his own collection as well as those from two of his friends. My colleague Pete Brabham has performed digital wizardry by breathing life into a couple of images that were showing signs of their age. Many thanks also to Paul Hood and Bob Allen, for their help and useful comments. As always Gil Mayes has willingly read draft pages and we have gained much from his extensive knowledge and Bernard McCall has provided valuable guidance throughout the project. Written sources used are numerous and include various volumes of *Lloyds Register of Shipping*, various editions of *Ian Allan Ocean Ships* and *ABC Ocean Tankers*, *Merchant Ships World Built*, *The British Tankers*, *Sea Shell* and various *World Ship Society* publications, as well as *Ships Monthly* magazine.

Andrew Wiltshire   **Cardiff, June 2008**

Published by Bernard McCall, 400 Nore Road, Portishead, Bristol, BS20 8EZ, England. Website : www.coastalshipping.co.uk
Telephone/fax : 01275 846178. E-mail : bernard@coastalshipping.co.uk
All distribution enquiries should be addressed to the publisher.

Printed by Amadeus Press, Ezra House, West 26 Business Park, Cleckheaton, West Yorkshire, BD19 4TQ
Telephone : 01274 863210; fax : 01274 863211; e-mail : info@amadeuspress.co.uk; website : www.amadeuspress.co.uk

ISBN : 928-1-902953-36-6

Front cover: The **Crania**, **Camitia** and **Cinulia** were a trio of similar motor tankers built specifically for carrying lubricating oil products. They were intended for trading between Venezuela, Curacao and northern Europe. The **Crania**, seen here on the Manchester Ship Canal at Runcorn, was completed in May 1955 for Shell Tankers N.V. and sailed under the Dutch flag. She was a regular visitor to the Canal with lubricants for Shell's Stanlow refinery. Her dimensions also allowed her to handle cargoes at the grease plant further along the Canal at Barton. The **Crania** was constructed by C. v.d. Giessen, of Krimpen. and was 9094grt. She had an overall length of 501 feet and a breadth of 62 feet. Her 5-cylinder B & W engine of 4600bhp was built by N.V. Mch. & Schps P Smit Jr and gave her a speed of 13 knots. She had thirty cargo tanks all with heating coils. The **Crania** was sold to Lien Ho Hsing Steel Enterprises of Kaohsiung for scrap in May 1984. Her two sisterships also ended their days in the Far East being broken up in the mid-1980s.

(Eddie Jackson)

Back cover: Despite her appalling external condition, the Liberian flag **Palouse** of 1955 makes a somewhat attractive subject in the near perfect and tranquil setting of the River Fal in Cornwall. The date is 6 September 1976 and just six months later the **Palouse** will be laying at the breakers yard at Bilbao. This tanker, yet another of traditional layout, was launched as the Norwegian-owned **Kongstein** by Kockums yard at Malmö in Sweden. Her owner, Brodrene Olsen A/S had specified a motor ship with a 9-cylinder M.A.N. type diesel which was built by the shipyard. The output of 8100bhp gave her a speed of around 14 knots. Her principal dimensions were 15828grt, 24420dwt, 606 feet overall length, 77 feet beam and maximum draught of 32 feet. She changed hands just twice in her career. In 1968 she became the **Capetan Lukis** for Cia. Laconia de Nav, of Monrovia, and finally the **Palouse** in 1974. As such she sailed for Palouse Shipping Ltd also under the Liberian flag. She arrived at Bilbao on 1 March 1977 for breaking up.

(John Wiltshire)

I shall commence by taking a look at some ocean-going tankers from a few British flag fleets. The attractive British tanker **Stonegate** was based upon Shell's A class of three-island layout products carriers. She was originally ordered by Shell but was delivered to Turnbull Scott Shipping Co Ltd, with a long term charter to Shell being part of the deal. She was completed in March 1961 and was delivered from Smith's Dock Company's yard at South Bank on the River Tees. The **Stonegate** was 12270 grt and had 33 cargo tanks. She was a motor tanker powered by a Hawthorn Leslie built Doxford oil engine of 8000bhp. The **Stonegate** joined the turbine tanker **Eastgate** (of 1955) on long term charter to Shell. Unfortunately the ill-fated **Eastgate**, which was based upon Shell's H class, was burnt out after a collision in 1973. The **Stonegate** was sold in 1981 and saw further service as the **Sunny** of Cyclamina Cia. Nav S.A. sailing under the Cypriot flag. She was broken up at Chittagong, arriving there on 1 May 1987. Here we see her underway in the Crosby Channel on the River Mersey, on 28 May 1978.

(Paul Boot)

An equal partnership between BP and Houlder Brothers was established in 1958 and was registered as The Warwick Tanker Co Ltd. Two 37000dwt tankers were ordered for delivery in 1960 and would be chartered to BP for a period of fifteen years. They were named **Brandon Priory** built by Hawthorn, Leslie at Hebburn and **Bidford Priory** from the Cammell Laird shipyard at Birkenhead. Their funnels were based on the normal Houlder Bros funnel marking, but with the addition of the BP Shield placed over the Maltese cross. The **Brandon Priory** is seen here on the Tyne on 30 May 1961, a location where she would be drydocked and receive repairs. Intended to carry crude oil, she had 10 centre tanks with a similar number of wing tanks to port and starboard. She was powered by double reduction geared steam turbines with an output of 15500shp which gave her a speed of 16 knots. Her 15-year charter expired in 1975 and in February of that year she suffered an engine room fire whilst off Port Elizabeth, South Africa. The **Brandon Priory** was not to see further service beyond 1975 as she was sold to breakers at Castellon in Spain in June of that year. Her sistership **Bidford Priory** met a similar end at Faslane in October 1975.

(Malcolm Donnelly)

Athel Line Ltd was owned by the United Molasses Company and operated a fleet of ocean-going tankers. The **Athelcrown** was a molasses tanker. These tankers would obtain their cargoes in places such as Mauritius, the Caribbean and later Brazil. In the United Kingdom, Athel had storage tank facilities at ports including Avonmouth, Birkenhead and Hull. In later years the main use for molasses was as a binding additive in cattle feed. The **Athelcrown** was launched on 15 February 1949 by Cammell Laird Shipbuilders at Birkenhead. She was 11149grt and was registered in Liverpool upon completion the following June. She was a motor ship,

her main engine being a 4-cylinder Doxford of 4450bhp which gave her a sea speed of 11 knots. She had three sisterships in the Athel Line fleet, the **Athellaird** also of 1949 and the 1950-built **Athelking** and **Athelmonarch**. The **Athelcrown** is seen at Cardiff in August 1969 bathed in late evening sunshine, having just been released from the Channel Drydock. Her life as a molasses tanker was to end in December 1971 when she arrived at Burriana in Spain to be broken up.

(Bob Allen)

The 13105grt *Thirlby* was a typical motor tanker of the 1950s and was constructed by Sir J Laing and Sons Ltd at their Deptford Yard in Sunderland for the Ropner Shipping Co Ltd. The ship owning company Ropner came into being in 1874 based in West Hartlepool. Despite heavy losses in both World Wars, the company continued to trade until taken over by Jacobs Holdings in the 1990s. The *Thirlby* was launched on 2 May 1958 and completed in the following October. She had a 6-cylinder Doxford 2-stroke opposed piston engine of 8000bhp and a service speed of 14 knots. The *Thirlby* would put in an impressive 23 years service for her owner on unbroken charter to Shell Tankers. She was sold in 1981 and became the *Diamando* of the Dioskouri Shipping Company sailing under the Greek flag. Her useful life over, she was broken up at Aliaga in Turkey in late 1984. She is seen here on the River Tees in January 1976, the weak sunshine just picking out her green hull.

(John Wiltshire collection)

The *Malwa* was launched on 30 May 1961 at Barrow-in-Furness by Vickers-Armstrong Ltd. She was delivered to Charter Shipping Co Ltd (a Bermudan subsidiary of P & O), and placed in service in P & O house colours with a black funnel. At 24266grt and 37278dwt, she was the first of the P & O Group's eight 37000dwt tankers to have all her accommodation placed aft. The first five tankers in this series are of the more conventional layout, with wheelhouse and officers' accommodation mid-ships. In 1963 Trident Tankers became managers and then became her owners in 1971. She is seen here in Trident colours. The *Malwa* was a steam powered vessel, her main plant consisting of two steam turbines geared to a single shaft with an output of 16000shp. In this view she is swinging off the entrance to the Albert Edward Dock, North Shields, on 31 July 1969. She will then depart the River Tyne bound for the Persian Gulf. The *Malwa* had just been drydocked at Smiths Dock, North Shields. She had a relatively short service life and was sold to Chou's Iron and Steel Co Ltd, Kaohsiung, on 12 October 1975. Demolition work commenced in February 1976.

(Bernard Kent)

The BP Tanker Co Ltd placed orders for a total of fourteen 16000dwt products tankers which would become known as the "Bird" class. The **British Fulmar** is seen passing along the New Waterway on 14 July 1975. She was one of two "Bird" class tankers built on the Clyde by Alexander Stephen & Sons, of Glasgow, the other being the **British Curlew** of 1960. She was completed as 11169grt and was 524 feet overall length with a laden draught of 30 feet 1 inch. Her main engine was a 7-cylinder Sulzer of 8750bhp built under licence by the shipyard. The **British Fulmar** initially operated for the subsidiary Clyde Charter Company, being transferred to the BP Tanker Co Ltd in 1972. During her days with BP she could be classed as a tanker trading worldwide. In the late 1960s and early 1970s the **British Fulmar** visited such places as Bombay, Fremantle, Bandar Mahshahr and Cardiff. She was sold in 1976 to United Freighter Corp. Panama S.A. becoming **Zhujiang** under the Panamanian flag. She then became **Da Qing 236** in 1979 under the flag of the People's Republic of China. As such she sank 115 nautical miles north-east of Hong Kong on 11 October 1983, following a collision with an Indonesian freighter named **Gunung Klabat**.

(C C Beazley)

The **Volvatella** was one of twelve similar V Class crude oil carriers built for the Shell Group between 1950 and 1957. The first four appeared between 1950 and 1952 and were very slightly smaller. Other examples of similar dimensions to the **Volvatella** were the **Vibex** of 1955 and the **Volvula** of 1956. Of the twelve, two were to be found sailing under the Dutch flag. The **Volvatella** is seen on 16 September 1963 passing South Shields inbound, looking somewhat the worse for wear. She was built by Hawthorn, Leslie at Hebburn on Tyneside, and was completed in December 1956 for Shell Bermuda (Overseas) Ltd, London. She was 659ft in length and 84ft in the beam. Her gross tonnage was 20801grt and her original deadweight tonnage was 32308dwt which was to change to 33891 at some point between 1966 and 1972 and by 1975 had changed again to 34435dwt. All twelve tankers in this class were steam turbine powered, and the **Volvatella** had machinery assembled by the associated Hawthorn, Leslie (Engineering) Ltd. With an output of 14500shp this gave her a service speed of 15 knots. She was eventually retired and broken up at Tadotsu in Japan in 1975.

(Malcolm Donnelly)

The Italian-built **Esso Dublin** was completed in May 1960 for the Esso Petroleum Company. She was registered in London under the British flag and was a steam turbine tanker. The **Esso Dublin** was one of twelve similar 36000dwt tankers for Esso which were known as the "City" class. The first of these was the **Esso Guildford** built in Germany in 1957, the **Esso Dublin** being the last in the series. She was launched on 4 October 1959 at the yard of Cantieri Riuniti del' Adriatico at Monfalcone. She had a pair of geared turbines of 16000shp which gave her a service speed of 16 knots. She was 23720grt and 690 feet in length. In 1964 the **Esso Dublin** was transferred to the Esso Transport Company Inc, of Panama, and renamed **Esso Honduras**. As such she was sold for breaking up at Kaohsiung in June 1976. We see her here on the River Tyne, where she has been the recipient of a considerable quantity of fresh paint.

(Malcolm Donnelly)

The first tanker in a series of seventeen 18000dwt tankers was the **Abida**, built in the Netherlands in 1958 for the Royal Dutch Shell Group. This class became known as the Shell A class. Two vessels, the **Aluco** and **Arianta**, had all their accommodation placed aft. The **Abida** and three others were motor ships, the remainder were steam turbine tankers. One such turbine ship was the 12321grt **Aulica** of 1960. She was built by Kieler Howaldtswerke, of Kiel, for Tanker Finance Ltd, part of the Shell Group. The **Aulica** had a pair of geared turbines of 7500shp built by Howaldtswerke Hamburg A.G. which would give her a speed of 14 knots.

The A class of tankers had a number of improved design features over the earlier H and K class ships. As well as having a modern streamlined profile, they featured a much clearer working deck, with fewer hatches over the cargo tanks. Here the **Aulica** heads out into the Bristol Channel from Barry in very dramatic lighting on 22 September 1973. Storm clouds have already gathered in the background. The **Aulica** was at this time employed on UK coasting. She was delivered to Gadani Beach on 20 December 1984 for scrapping.

(Bob Allen)

In the early post-war years the British Tanker Co Ltd made it a priority to expand its fleet to that of pre-war levels. This was to match the increased oil production at Abadan in the Middle East. The years between 1945 and 1951 saw a total of fifty-four 12250dwt tankers constructed for the company. This size of vessel was at the time considered to be a useful size for general trading. A 1949-built example was the **British Liberty**, one of eight to be completed in Sunderland at the Pallion yard of Wm. Doxford. Other examples included the **British Major** of 1946 and the **British Builder** of 1951. The **British Liberty**, the second tanker to carry this name, was launched on 2 September 1948 and completed on 5 May 1949. She had a gross tonnage of 8589grt and overall length of just under 490 feet. Her main engine was a 4-cylinder Doxford 2-stroke diesel. Most of this class were replaced by larger tankers after about fifteen years of service. The **British Liberty** met her end in the Far East. She arrived at Hong Kong in tow on 27 June 1964 for breaking up.

(Malcolm Donnelly)

Moored adjacent to the Hawthorn, Leslie shipyard at Hebburn on 18 February 1961 is the **Kayeson**. She is fitting out for Kaye and Son (Kaye Tanker Management), and was handed over to her owners the following month. Kaye and Son had been associated with Royal Mail Steam Packet and Furness Withy since 1918, and was eventually absorbed into the Furness Withy Group in 1973 but still remained managers of this vessel. The **Kayeson** was a steam turbine tanker of 28132grt and 47941dwt. Her two geared steam turbines were manufactured by her builder Hawthorn, Leslie and with an output of 16000shp gave her a speed of 16 knots. By 1975 her registered owners were Royal Mail Lines Ltd with Kaye Tanker Management as her managers. The **Kayeson** was the last vessel to bear the colours of her original owners and was sold for further trading in 1981. As the **Aounallah** she sailed under the Panamanian flag until May 1983. At this point she arrived at Gadani Beach in Pakistan for breaking up.

(Bernard Kent)

A large number of tankers could be found sailing under the flags of Scandinavian countries and we now look at some of these. The Norwegian flagged **Wilhelm Jebsen** is seen arriving off Avonmouth with a cargo of refined products on 8 June 1969. She was a motor tanker built in the United Kingdom for A/R Caloric with Paul Jebsen acting as manager. Launched at Newcastle on 10 July 1953 she was a product of the Neptune yard of Swan, Hunter and Wigham Richardson Ltd. The

Wilhelm Jebsen was 12303grt and 537 feet in length by 73 feet in the beam. She was powered by a 6-cylinder Doxford engine (of 7500bhp) built under licence by Swan Hunter which gave her a speed of 14.5 knots. Her owner when seen in this view is described as A/R Seljan and A/R Atlantic and she is registered in Bergen. She went on to become the **Telenikis** in 1971 under the Cypriot flag and was broken up at Barcelona during 1976.

(John Wiltshire)

The Finnish flagged tanker *Tervi* was designed with a requirement to transport oil over short distances, mainly in the Baltic. As such, she had to be equipped with high specification loading and discharge facilities and had to be highly manoeuvrable. To this end she was capable of discharging her cargo in under seven hours. She had a controllable-pitch propeller and a 500hp bow-thruster unit to assist her in and out of port. Perhaps her most distinctive feature is her oval-shaped wheelhouse that has windows through a full 360 degrees. The *Tervi* was a motor ship built in 1963 by Rauma-Repola OY for Neste OY. She was 11121grt and 537 feet overall length. She had an 8-cylinder Gotaverken diesel of 6650bhp. The *Tervi* had a hull designed to navigate in ice, and in open water could achieve 14.5 knots. Neste OY was established in 1948 to oversee Finland's oil import and refining industry. and purchased its first tanker in 1948. The *Tervi* became the *Jussara* under the Greek flag in 1984, and was broken up at Alang in June 2003 after 40 years service. She is being towed towards the Queen Alexandra lock at Cardiff on 22 October 1978, having discharged a cargo of mainly petroleum and diesel oil at the Gulf oil terminal in the Roath Dock.

(John Wiltshire)

Another Finnish flagged tanker, but this time a little older, is the **Passad III** of 1955. She was delivered to the Swedish company Rederi A/B Tankoil as **Nike** in June 1955. She had been launched by the Swedish shipbuilder A/B Gotaverken of Gothenburg three months earlier in March. Her principal dimensions were 593 feet in length with a breadth of 75 feet. Her tonnages are given as 14778grt and 23979dwt. In 1967 the **Nike** became the **Annika Smith** and in 1968 she changed hands once again becoming the **Passad III** of A/B Helsingfors Steamship Co Ltd. She is seen here in the oil dock at Avonmouth on 30 October 1971. Her hull is in need of some fresh paint. The **Passad III** was broken up at San Esteban de Pravia in northern Spain by Desguarces y Recuperanciones del Norte S.A. in 1976.

(John Wiltshire)

Messrs Fearnley and Eger were cousins who set up as partners as long ago as 1872. As ship owners they bought their first tanker in 1928. In April 1958 the company took delivery of the **Fernhaven**, the first ship in the fleet to carry this name. The **Fernhaven** is seen sailing unladen from Barry on an early evening high water in 1966, having just discharged a cargo at the port. The **Fernhaven** is another example of a Norwegian tanker constructed in the UK. She was built on the Clyde by Charles Connell and Co Ltd, of Scotstoun. Her principal dimensions were 12689grt and 18610dwt. She was 556 feet in length and 73 feet in the beam. Her 6-cylinder Doxford engine built under licence by Barclay, Curle and Co Ltd gave her a maximum sea speed of 14 knots. Her delivery followed on from the similar **Fernstar** of 1955, also from the same yard on the Clyde. In 1967 the **Fernhaven** was sold to Italian buyers Marsud SpA who registered her at Palermo bearing the name **Polluce**. As such she caught fire near Cape Corso in June 1981. She was bound for Genoa and was in ballast. She was salvaged and towed to Livorno. Eventually declared a total loss, she was broken up at La Spezia in 1982.

(Bob Allen)

The Norwegian flagged **Thordis** is seen in June 1971 at Avonmouth. She is leaving her berth in the oil dock having discharged a consignment of products including petroleum. She was built for Tønnevolds Rederi A/S and is in her final year of service for them. She would become the **Thomas** of Lorentzens Kysttank R/A later in 1971. The **Thordis** was built at Gothenburg by Gotaverken in 1955. She was a motor ship of 11005grt and 17400dwt. She was 549 feet in length and had a speed of 14 knots. In 1973 she was purchased by Kea Shipping Corporation under the management of North Atlantic Shipping Agency Ltd, of London. At this point her aft section was joined to the bow and cargo section of the tanker **Brussels** (originally the **Caltex Brussels** of 1951) to form a new ship. This work was carried out by the Hong Kong United Dockyards Ltd. The new vessel was then renamed **Knassos** under the Liberian flag. A further change of name occurred in 1974 when she became the **Souli** and still sailing for Kea Shipping. Four years later it was all over for this "jumbo-ised" vessel, and she was reduced to scrap by Spanish ship-breakers at Bilbao.

(Bob Allen)

The appropriately-named motor tanker **Panama** is seen passing along the Panama Canal with the tug **Alianza** in attendance. Built in 1977 by A/S Nakskov Skibsvaerft of Nakskov, Denmark, the **Panama** and her sister the **Paranagua** sailed under the Danish flag for the East Asiatic Co Ltd. This view of her gives us an excellent view of the layout of her deck space. Built as a products carrier, her cargo section consisted of twenty-four tanks some of which could carry Type C chemicals. Her four cargo pumps had a capacity of 900 cubic metres per hour. The **Panama** had a gross tonnage of 20943grt, a length of 560 feet and a draught of 38 feet when fully laden. Her main engine was a 6-cylinder Burmeister & Wain 6K74EF, which produced 12500bhp at 134rpm. The vessel was sold a number of times in her career and became the **Capri Alfa** in 1988. She had six further name changes between 1989 and 2001. It was then she finally became the **Norsea** under the Maltese flag but with an Italian owner and Norwegian manager. She was still sailing as the **Norsea** in 2003, but then with Greek owners. This thirty one year old tanker was finally broken up at Alang in February 2007.

(David Oldham collection)

Texaco Norway A/S, of Oslo, operated the elegant motor tanker **Texaco Norge** which was delivered in July 1962. She was built at Fredrikstad by A/S Fredrikstad mek Verksted and had a 7-cylinder Gotaverken diesel of 8750bhp. Her sistership was the **Texaco Skandinavia**. The **Texaco Norge** had a gross tonnage of 13233 and was 578 feet overall length. As can be seen she was of conventional layout with clean lines to her hull and superstructure. Texaco was one of a number of tanker operators that used to advertise their business in large letters on the hull,

as can be seen here. After twenty-four years service with her original owner, she was sold in 1986 to the Getty Marine Corporation (Texaco Marine Services Inc.) and placed under the Bahamas flag. Retaining the name **Texaco Norge** she sailed for two more years before arriving at Kaohsiung on 6 June 1988. A week later Kuo Dar Enterprises Co Ltd began to break her up for scrap. She is seen here on the New Waterway in May 1971.

(Bob Allen)

Many tankers could be found sailing under Greek, Liberian or Panamanian flags of convenience and our attention now turns to a selection of these. The Liberian flagged **Fortuity** was built as the **Border Regiment** in 1953, the first of a class of ten similar vessels for the Lowland Tanker Co Ltd, of Newcastle. They were managed by Common Bros who had a 25% share in the ships, Jardine Matheson & Co also had 25% and BP held the remaining 50%. She was launched on 4 November 1952 by Scotts' Shipbuilding Co Ltd, of Greenock, and completed the following March. She was a motor tanker of 11331grt and 15950 dwt. Her builders constructed her 6-cylinder Doxford type engine which had an output of 7040bhp. Her cargo tank capacity was 747,265 cubic feet. She gained the name **Fortuity** in 1969 having been sold to Fortuity Cia. Nav S.A. and was placed under the Liberian flag. As such she made her final voyage to ship-breakers at Pusan, South Korea, in February 1975. Here we see her arriving at Avonmouth on 30 October 1971. An interesting feature of this class of tanker was the tripod mast above the wheelhouse.

(John Wiltshire)

The **Georgian Valour** is seen in August 1971 at Sunderland, where she was built eighteen years earlier. She is laid up, having arrived at the port in the previous February with damage. She was built by Wm Doxford at their Pallion yard. She was launched on 14 April 1953 as the **Sylvafield** for Northern Petroleum Tank S.S. Co Ltd, with Hunting & Son Ltd as managers. She was a motor tanker of 11243grt with a 6-cylinder Doxford main engine of 7750bhp. The **Sylvafield** was similar in many respects to the **Avonfield** also dating from 1953. The **Sylvafield** became the **Georgian Valour** in 1969 for the Pantheon Corporation and placed under the Liberian flag. After arrival at Sunderland she was destined never to sail again commercially. The **Georgian Valour** arrived at Bilbao on 16 September 1971 for breaking by Hierros Ardes, who had paid in the region of £86,000 for her. Demolition commenced by 18 October.

(Roy Cressey)

A fully-laden **Esso Bayway** is seen making slow progress along the New Waterway on 28 June 1976. Of interest are the enclosed lifeboats and the large angular gantry structure ahead of her funnel serving the machinery space below. Despite the impressive size of this funnel, she is in fact a motor ship built in Japan in 1974 by Hitachi Zosen of Mukaishima. Her main engine is a 7-cylinder Burmeister & Wain built under licence by Hitachi Zosen with an output of 9400bhp. The **Esso Bayway** has thirteen tanks all fitted with steam heating coils. Her gross tonnage is 12805grt and she was capable of 15 knots. Her owner from new was Esso Tankers Inc, New York, and she flew the Liberian flag. She was replaced in 1978 by a similar size vessel with the same name. The **Esso Bayway** was then transferred to Esso Sociedad Anonima Petrolera Argentina, of Buenos Aires, as **Petromar Campana II**. After two further changes of name she became **Al Madina** in 1995. She continued to trade until 2000 when she was sold for scrap and broken up at Alang.

(John Wiltshire collection)

The **Varkiza** was a Greek flagged tanker of 12302grt and is seen here lying in Piraeus Roads on 23 December 1997. She is starting to show signs of her age. She was originally built in Poland in 1968 as the **Talsy**. The **Talsy** was a B70 type tanker built at Gdynia for the U.S.S.R. Government by Stocznia im Komuny Paryskiej. Her main engine was a 6-cylinder Sulzer of 9600bhp assembled by H. Cegielski. She sailed under the Russian flag until 1990 when she was sold to Mantinia Shipping Co. S.A., of Piraeus, and named **Varkiza** under the flag of Malta. However, by 1992 she was sailing for Varkiza Naftiki Eteria under Greek registry. Her final years of trading saw her active in Greek waters, plying between such ports as Piraeus, Thessaloniki and Heraklion. The **Varkiza** bowed out in 1999. She passed to St. Vincent and The Grenadines flag interests, was renamed **Ark**, and subsequently delivered to breakers at Alang on 25 November 1999.

(Nigel Jones)

Built for the Monrovia Tanker Company, of Monrovia, in 1960, the **Mary Livanos** was destined to sail for eighteen years without a change of name or owner. She was a Dutch-built steam turbine tanker sailing under the Liberian flag. Her builders were Wilton-Fijenoord, of Schiedam, from whose yard she was launched on 10 March 1960. The **Mary Livanos** was 13742grt and 19500dwt and was 565 feet in length and 74 feet breadth. Her two geared turbines produced 8250ihp which gave her a service speed of 15 knots. This view shows her arriving at Barry with a part cargo on 22 September 1973. This would have included oil of various grades such as petroleum, diesel, furnace oil and possibly even some vegetable oils. Her end came when she arrived at Kaohsiung in May 1978 for reduction to scrap.

(Bob Allen)

The **Eleni V** is one of those ships that many people would prefer to forget about. She began life as the **Scottish Ptarmigan** of the Scottish Tanker Co Ltd (with Huntley, Cook & Co Ltd as managers) in 1958. She was built by John Brown & Co (Clydebank) Ltd and powered by a 6-cylinder Doxford oil engine manufactured by John Brown. She was 12685grt and had nine main centre tanks and sixteen wing tanks. In 1968 she became the **Markab** of Compania Naviera Alheli SA Monrovia and sailed under the Liberian flag. In 1970 she was bought by N J Vardinoyannis, of Piraeus, who renamed her **Eleni V**. On 6 May 1978 the **Eleni V** was on passage from Rotterdam to Grangemouth laden with 16,000 tons of heavy fuel oil. In thick fog and six miles off Winterton, Great Yarmouth, she was in collision with the French bulk carrier **Roseline** (16023grt/1974). The **Eleni V** was sliced into two, but miraculously her tanks remained intact. The aft section was towed safely away but her bow section rolled over and drifted off leaking oil. It was later blown up by a team of Royal Navy divers 10 days later and 25 miles offshore. There was extensive pollution along the Suffolk and Norfolk coastline. The **Eleni V** is seen at Cardiff on 24 August 1973.

(John Wiltshire)

The immaculate Greek flagged tanker **Pavlos V.** is seen here awaiting orders in Piraeus Roads on 2 September 1985. She is owned by Universal Peace Shipping Enterprises of Piraeus and dates from 1958. Launched as the **Floreal** by the Danish yard of Odense Staalskibsværft A/S of Odense, she was delivered new to Soc. Des Transports Maritimes Petroliers (TMP). She sailed under the French flag, along with her sistership **Longchamp** also of 1958. She was a motor tanker of 18587grt and 29542dwt. The **Floreal** had 24 cargo tanks and her main engine was a 10-cylinder Burmeister & Wain diesel of 13900bhp. She was sold in 1968 becoming the **Matheos** under the Greek flag. She gained three more names, including the distinctive title **Thomas G. Chimples** before finally becoming the **Pavlos V.** in 1978. She appears to be kept in good order, and this may have helped ensure her survival for a further eight years after this photograph was taken. She eventually met her fate after arriving at Gadani Beach on 21 May 1993.

(Bob Allen)

Completed in 1979 by Mitsubishi Heavy Industry Ltd, of Nagasaki, for the Chevron Transport Corporation, the **Kenneth E. Hill** was a large tanker of 43428grt and 81273dwt. Her dimensions stood at 820 feet length by 144 feet breadth with a maximum draught of 40 feet. She sailed under the Liberian flag and when photographed departing from Milford Haven, her hull seemed to be in need of some cosmetic attention. The **Kenneth E. Hill** was a motor ship capable of 16 knots and was powered by a 20300bhp Sulzer diesel which had been built under licence by the shipyard in Japan. She had one sistership, the **William E. Mussman** also of 1979. The **Kenneth E. Hill** was destined to be a Chevron tanker throughout her whole career and was reported to have been broken up at Jiangyin in China some time around May 2002.

(Bernard McCall)

We shall now take a look at tankers at various locations around the world. The **British Esk** was one of a dozen "River" class tankers built for the BP Tanker Co Ltd in the early 1970s. They emerged from no fewer than five different shipyards. The **British Esk** was delivered in September 1973 from the Belgian yard of N.V. Boelwerf S.A. at Tamise. This yard also built the **British Tamar**, **British Test** and **British Trent**. She was a motor vessel of 15644grt and 562 feet in overall length. Her first real claim to fame came in April 1982 when she was one of eight "River"

class to be requisitioned by the MoD for use in the Falklands Conflict. As part of the Falklands Task Force she was chartered to the Royal Fleet Auxiliary. The **British Esk** is seen here lying at anchor in Singapore Roads on 18 June 1997. She was then owned by BP Shipping Bermuda Ltd and carried the later BP funnel colours. She was also notable as being the training ship for engineering cadets for the BP fleet. Only ever trading as the **British Esk**, she was sold to Chinese breakers at Xinhui in early 2001.

(Nigel Jones)

Imperial Oil opened a refinery at Sarnia, Ontario, in 1897. In 1948 they took delivery of a fine looking steam tanker, the **Imperial Sarnia**. Her duties were to include the shipment of crude oil from Superior in Wisconsin to the Sarnia refinery, and the supply of refined products to installations on the Great Lakes. She was constructed by Collingwood Shipyards Ltd, of Collingwood, Ontario, and was originally 4580grt. The **Imperial Sarnia** was a single-screw steam turbine powered tanker. She was rebuilt in 1954 at Sorel, which included lengthening her hull. After being rebuilt her tonnages changed to 4947grt with a deadweight of 6832dwt. She

was transferred to take up service on Canada's east coast and for this duty she was based at Halifax. In the summer of 1965 she returned to Great Lakes service and was due to be retired in 1973. However, the **Imperial Sarnia** was reprieved, and went on to give several more years of service. After withdrawal from active service she became a static moored oil storage vessel at Hamilton by 1986, and carried the name **Provmar Terminal II**. Towards the end of her active years, she is seen laying over on the Welland Ship Canal on 13 June 1983.

(Bob Allen)

The career of this French tanker was to span eighteen years. The **Port Vendres** was launched on 19 April 1958 from the yard of At. & Ch. de la Seine Maritime at Le Trait located downstream from Rouen on the River Seine. She was constructed for the account of Socété d'Armement Fluvial et Maritime (SOFLUMAR) and registered at Dunkerque. At 9289grt and 14519dwt, she was a handy-sized tanker with an overall length of 511 feet. She was powered by a 6-cylinder 2-stroke B&W diesel of 5400bhp, manufactured by Ch. de l'Atlantique and this gave her a speed of 14 knots. The **Port Vendres** is seen here heading down the New Waterway on a very pleasant 6 May 1975. Less than twelve months later she would arrive at Gijon in northern Spain in February 1976 to be broken up.

(Paul Boot)

The steam tanker **Evmits** is seen in very good condition passing Perama near Piraeus on 6 October 1981. The photographer was enjoying a Thames Ship Society trip to the area. This vessel was completed in 1960 as **Caroline Maersk** for Danish ship owner A P Møller Ltd. Prior to this on 14 November 1959 she was launched as **Caroline**. Her Danish builders were Odense Staalskibsværft A/S and she was 24532grt and 39325dwt. At the time of her delivery she was the largest ship to have been built in Denmark. She had a large cargo pump just ahead of the engine room and a smaller one just aft of her fo'c'sle. The **Caroline Maersk** had a

pair of double reduction geared steam turbines by the General Electric Co. With an output of 13750shp she had a service speed of 15 knots. She was followed into service by an identical tanker the **Katrine Maersk** of 1961. Sold by A P Møller in 1971, she became **E.M. Tsangaris** before passing to Evmits Tankers Inc, London & Piraeus, in 1979. They renamed her **Evmits** under the Greek flag. She was broken up at Castellon in Spain, arriving there on 28 February 1983.

(Bob Allen)

This ship began life as the **Asia** in 1959 with the well-known Danish ship owner the East Asiatic Company. She had two sisterships, the **Annam** of 1958 and **Java** of 1960. She was delivered on 12 March 1959 by her builders, Nakskov Skibsværft. She was 12499grt and had a service speed of 16 knots. Her main engine was a Burmeister and Wain 2-stroke single acting oil engine of 10000bhp. The **Asia** only served the East Asiatic Company for about a year. She was sold in February 1960 to D.B. Deniz Nakliyati T.A.S, Istanbul, and renamed **Garzan** under the Turkish flag. Apparently she was handed over to her new owners at Galveston, Texas. The **Garzan** is seen here in Istanbul Roads, date unknown. Her funnel appears unusually large for a motor tanker. The history of her later years remains patchy. We do know that she passed to Turkish ship-breakers at Aliaga in 1985.

(David Oldham collection)

Seen sailing from the South African port of Durban in 1986 is the elderly Panamanian flagged motor tanker **Acuario Diez**. Here we see her in her forty sixth year, having been built in Sweden as long ago as 1940. She was ordered from the yard of Oresundsvarvet A/B at Landskrona for A/S Rendal, of Oslo, but was actually delivered in July 1940 to Rederi-A/B Dalen of Gothenburg as the **Glomdal**. By 1946 she was sailing under the Portuguese flag as the **Aire** and passed to Spanish owners as the **Ciudad Rodrigo** in 1952. It would appear that her 15 cargo tanks were renewed in 1962. It was not until 1984 that she changed hands once again passing to Buques Marisqueros as the **Acuario Diez**. She was 3942grt and retained her original engine all her life, a 1932 vintage Sulzer Bros diesel of 1500bhp. She arrived at Seville for breaking up in July 1987. Her final owner was given as Somasped S.A. of Panama.

(Roy Cressey collection)

The ***Chilbar*** is a US flagged tanker that has been subject to major surgery. The aft section originates from 1959, launched as the ***Eagle Traveler*** by Ingalls Shipbuilding Corporation, of Pascagoula. She was originally a type T5-S-41A tanker and was second of a pair built for Sea Transport Corporation of Wilmington. She had a pair of double-reduction geared steam turbines supplied by Westinghouse Electric Corporation. These drove a single screw and gave her a speed of 17 knots. In 1981 her forward and cargo section was scrapped and a new section of hull was constructed by Newport News Shipbuilding and Drydock Co, and joined to the remaining part of the ship. Her new overall length was actually reduced slightly to 665 feet but her breadth increased from 84 feet to 102 feet. The tanker was now registered as 19291grt and 34223dwt. Her owners were Chilbar Shipping Co (Keystone Shipping Co, managers) and she was registered in Wilmington. Renamed ***Chilbar***, she would become a U.S. coastal oil/chemical tanker for the next 23 years, trading mainly in the U.S. Gulf area. She is caught by the camera underway on the Houston Ship Canal on 26 September 1996. The ***Chilbar*** was eventually sold to Indian ship-breakers in 2005, arriving at Alang in February of the same year.

(Nigel Jones)

The West German yard of Bremer Vulkan AG, of Vegesack near Bremen, launched the conventional motor tanker **Faust** on 24 March 1955 for Mobil Oil Reederei GmbH. She sailed as such until 1962 when she departed for new owners in Turkey. She became the **Mersin** under the German flag of Marmara Transport A.S. She was 11312grt with 27 cargo tanks and has been quoted as having accommodation for ten passengers. Her main engine was a 6-cylinder 2-stroke double-acting diesel of 6500bhp assembled by her builder. In 1993 the **Mersin** passed to Transpetrol Uluslarasi Denizcilik ve Ticaret A.S, of Istanbul, and remained under the Turkish flag. In 2000 she was sold to Cambodian flag owners and renamed **Mersi**. As such she arrived at Gadani Beach on 17 December 2000 for breaking up. This is where we see her a week later on 24 December.

(Nigel Jones)

The **Lumen** was built in Sweden in 1971 for the Cunard Steamship Co Ltd and was managed by Cunard-Brocklebank Ltd. In 1970 the activities of Cunard-Brocklebank, Port Line and Moss Tankers were incorporated into Cunard Cargo Shipping Services. This could explain why the **Lumen** carries the funnel colours of Moss Tankers. She was completed on 4 November 1971 by Eriksbergs M/V A/B, of Gothenburg, and was a motor ship of 14925grt and 25001dwt. She was one of five similar ships built between 1968 and 1972, which included the **Luminous** and the **Lumiere**. She had 33 tanks and was just under 557 feet in length. As a tanker the **Lumen** was quite advanced for her time. She featured a controllable pitch propeller which could push her along at 14 knots. The symbol on her hull just below the anchor tells us that she has a bulbous bow. Her main machinery consisted of two 12-cylinder vee type 4-stroke Lindholmens Motor Akt. (Pielstick) medium-speed diesels, geared to a single shaft with a total output of 10080bhp. The **Lumen** is seen here at an anchorage near Jeddah. She was sold to Al Dammam Navigation Co. Ltd in 1977 and became the **Al Dammam 1**. She later became the **Kriti Samaria** in 1984 under the Greek flag. Her final role was as the Italian **Egnazia**. She sailed as such from 1986 until February 1999 when she arrived at Alang for breaking up.

(Stan Tedford)

The **Maria Fassio** is yet another fine looking steam turbine tanker that was to sail without ever undergoing a name change. She was a pure Italian tanker being constructed at La Spezia by Ansaldo SpA, and completed in November 1960. The full title of her owner was Villain & Fassio e Cia. Internazionale di Genova Soc. Riunite di Nav. SpA. Despite her rather shabby appearance, she still makes a fine sight arriving here on the Mersey on 27 May 1974. Her most distinctive feature has to be her splendid funnel. The **Maria Fassio** had a gross tonnage of 21184 and was capable of 16 knots. What makes her story even more remarkable is that after seventeen years service she was to be broken up at the port of her construction, La Spezia, in April 1977.

(Paul Boot)

The **Gelendzhik** was a Russian-built motor tanker dating from 1957. She was one of a class of around 53 similar tankers and was built in the USSR as the **Stanislav**. She was launched in April 1957 from Admiralty 194 yard at Leningrad. She became **Gelendzhik** in 1974. In this view she is seen heading up the Bosphorus on 23 April 1981. At this time she was operating for the Novorossiysk Shipping Co of Russia and was regularly to be seen passing through the Bosphorus to and from such places as the Antarctic, Canaries and Italy. The **Gelendzhik** was 477 feet in length and with a gross tonnage of 7653. Power for propulsion was obtained from a pair of 8-cylinder Skoda diesel engines that were geared to a single propeller shaft. This gave her a service speed of just over 12 knots. She was broken up in Russia some time prior to December 1986.

(Nigel Jones)

The US flagged **Gulfsupreme** was launched on 22 August 1961 for the Gulf Oil Corporation and registered in Philadelphia. She was an attractive tanker built by the Bethlehem Steel Corporation of Sparrows Point in Maryland. She was the first vessel in the Gulf fleet to carry the new company emblem on her funnel, introduced in 1963. The **Gulfsupreme** was one of six similar steam turbine tankers built for Gulf. The others included the **Gulfspray** and **Gulfpride**. Her dimensions are given as 644 feet in length by 84 feet in the beam. She was 19030grt (31300dwt) and had a cargo capacity of 255,196 barrels, a term frequently used in the United States. In 1984 she was sold to become the **Coastal Manatee** of Coastal Manatee Inc, still under the US flag. She was to continue trading until late 1999, when she arrived at Chittagong for scrapping. She is seen here fully laden underway, thought to be near New Orleans, on the mighty Mississippi.

(Stan Tedford)

Our attention now turns to a visually impressive category of tanker, namely the VLCC (Very Large Crude Carrier) which had made its mark worldwide by the 1970s. The Esso Petroleum Company owned the VLCC **Esso Ulidia** seen here at Fawley on 13 May 1978. She was engaged on UK coasting duties at this time, and other terminals visited would include Milford Haven and Sullom Voe. The **Esso Ulidia** sailed under the British flag and was 126538grt and 254011dwt. She was built by Harland & Wolff Ltd of Belfast and was floated out of her building dock on 11 May 1970. Her hull was a massive 1143 feet in length and her overall breadth was 170 feet. Her machinery consisted of a pair of AEI steam turbines of 32000shp driving a single propeller. Like so many VLCCs of her time the **Esso Ulidia** became surplus to requirements after only thirteen years service. She was laid up on the Johore River between January and March 1983, and departed for breakers at Kaohsiung the following April. She arrived there for beaching and scrapping on 20 April.

(John Wiltshire)

The Shell tanker **Northia** makes a spectacular sight on the River Tees on 14 March 1998 resplendent with her immaculate red hull. She joined the Shell Tankers UK fleet as the **Northia** in 1980, when she was rebuilt for use as a North Sea Shuttle tanker. She began life in 1971 as the **Kronoland** for Swedish owner Brosstroms Rederi. She was built by Eriksbergs M/V A/B of Gothenberg and was 64815 grt when completed. In 1979 she became the **Oceanic Renown** of Sevenseas Tanker Transport Inc under the Liberian flag. Not technically a VLCC, but certainly a supertanker, she was a motor ship powered by a massive 25000bhp 10-cylinder Burmeister & Wain oil engine assembled by the shipyard. She had a controllable pitch propeller and a speed of 15 knots. In 2001 she was to undergo her final name change to date and became the **Ikdam** of Ikdam Production S.A. sailing under the Liberian flag. She was still sailing in 2007.

(Roy Cressey)

In 1973 a VLCC was ordered from China Shipbuilding Corp of Kaohsiung for Marine Transport Lines (Oswego) of Monrovia. On 18 November 1975 her keel was laid. Nearly two years later in June 1977 she was launched as **Burmah Endeavour** for Burmah Endeavour Ltd. She was placed under the British flag with Denholm Ship Management as managers. She would be followed in 1978 by the identical **Burmah Enterprise**. She was hailed as the third largest ship in the world at the time. Her statistics were impressive at 457,841dwt (231629grt), with an overall length of 1241 feet and extreme breadth of 223 feet. She had a pair of Ishikawajima (IHI) steam turbines geared to a single propeller shaft with an output of 45000shp. In 1983 Burmah Oil Tankers Ltd became her managers. She is seen here laid up at Southampton on 14 May 1983, and dwarfing the quayside behind her. After a long period of inactivity the **Burmah Endeavour** began trading again in June 1986, this time under the Bermudan flag. On 14 May 1988 whilst in use as a storage vessel at Hormuz Terminal, Laral Island, she was attacked by Iraqi aircraft and damaged. Later that year, once repaired, she was chartered to Stena Bulk Ab and renamed **Stena Queen**. In 1990 she was purchased by Stena and transferred to Royal Sky Shipping Ltd still under the Bermudan flag. Her final guise from 2002 was as the **Folk 1** and trading for Trans Shipping Saudi Arabia. On 9 April 2003 she was reported to be sailing from Kakinada bound for China to be broken up.

(John Wiltshire)

The VLCC **Hellespont Grand** started life in 1976 as the West German **Esso Deutschland** and sailed for Esso A.G. of Hamburg. She entered service on 7 October 1976 having been delivered by Kawasaki Heavy Industries Ltd of Sakaide in Japan. At 201658grt she was the largest vessel under the German flag at the time. Her overall length was 1235 feet and breadth was 226 feet. Naturally for a vessel of this size, her propulsion was steam consisting of a pair of turbines, geared to a single propeller shaft. The **Esso Deutschland** was laid up in a Norwegian fjord at Aalesund in March 1983 and was eventually sold in 1985 to the Grand Corporation of Liberia and renamed **Grand**. In 1990 she made her final change of name to **Hellespont Grand**, when she came under the ownership of Hellespont Grand Corp and was registered in the Marshall Islands. In her last decade she was still to be found trading worldwide visiting places such as the Bahamas, Singapore and Kharg Island in the Persian Gulf. The **Hellespont Grand** arrived in Greek waters at Eleusis on 14 June 2002 for lay up. We see her at Piraeus Roads just prior to this on 2 June. Once out of lay up, she was eventually to sail to Alang for breaking in early May 2003.

(Nigel Jones)

Seen making her way along the Suez Canal on 20 September 1994 is the **Kapetan Giorgis**, another former Esso VLCC. The Greek-owned **Kapetan Giorgis** was completed in Japan in 1977 as the **Esso Caribbean** for Esso Tankers Inc of Monrovia. She was initially launched as the **Andros Petros** by Ishikawajima-Harima Heavy Ind. (I.H.I.) of Kure in 1976 for a Liberian owner. The **Esso Caribbean** was 218447grt and 1241 feet in length. She had a draught of 82 feet when fully laden. Her builders assembled her two steam turbines which had an output of 45000shp and gave her a speed of 15 knots. She joined the **Esso Deutschland** (see page 38) in lay up at Aalesund in April 1983. Both had left lay up by 1986. The **Esso Caribbean** became the **Kapetan Giorgis** in 1990 when she was purchased by Presto Linea Inc. (Ceres Hellenic Shipping Enterprises Ltd). Under the Greek flag she was registered in Piraeus. She ended her days at Gadani Beach in the hands of Pakistani breakers, arriving there on 18 February 2002.

(Nigel Jones)

Our next section takes us to the Bristol Channel, a splendid place to see classic tankers in action. They could be noted with cargoes of refined products as well as in port for repairs and drydocking. The BP oil refinery at Llandarcy near Swansea would ensure that Swansea docks would always be a good place to see BP tankers. It was occasionally possible to see up to four at any one time in the Queen's Dock loading oil products. The **British Patrol** of 1954 was no stranger to the port. We see her about to enter the lock on 28 November 1969. She was an example of a class of twenty 16800dwt tankers constructed for the British Tanker Co Ltd. The **British Patrol** was the final example of five built by Swan, Hunter and

Wigham Richardson and was launched on 30 August 1954, and completed in the following November. She had four cargo pumps rated at 500 tons per hour, serving her 27 tanks. The **British Patrol** gave BP nineteen years service and was to be the only ship from this class of twenty to be sold for further service. She became the Cypriot-flagged **Maripatrol** in 1973, sailing for Marifoam Shipping Co Ltd (with Chandris as managers). In 1980 a further name change saw her sailing as **Nona Maro**. She was eventually broken up at Cartagena in the Spring of 1981.

(John Wiltshire)

40

A newer tanker for Texaco Norway A/S was the **Texaco Bergen** of 1977. She was launched on 12 January 1977 and completed four months later by A/S Horten Verft in Norway. She was 18378grt and 32006 dwt. Her main propulsion consisted of a 6-cylinder 2-stroke Sulzer diesel assembled by the shipyard. The **Texaco Bergen** featured a bulbous bow and a bow-thruster unit. She is seen here at Cardiff, still looking quite new on 15 August 1977. She had arrived with a cargo of motor spirit. In 1991 she was transferred to Texaco Marine Services Inc, of Port Arthur, and placed under the Bahamas flag as the **Star Bergen**. In 1993 her gross tonnage changed to 17679grt, and two years later she passed out of Texaco service. Her next name change occurred in 1999 when she became **Giannutri** of Giannutri Shipping Ltd under the Maltese flag. In 2002 she continued under the Maltese flag but as the Greek-owned **Minotaur**. Thanks to the fact that she has a double hull, she was still trading in 2008 registered in Barbados.

(Bob Allen)

The appearance of a Danish-flagged Esso tanker in the Bristol Channel was something of a novelty. The **Esso Callunda** is seen arriving at Cardiff on 11 June 1977 in somewhat gloomy lighting. She was owned by Dansk Esso A/S which at any one time, operated only a very small fleet of tankers. They deviated from normal Esso practice by incorporating buff in their funnel colours. The **Esso Callunda** was built in Japan by Hitachi Zosen, of Hiroshima, in 1974, and had a sistership, **Esso Hafnia**. Both were equipped with bow-thruster units. She was a 13503grt motor ship with 13 cargo tanks. Her overall length was 528 feet and her Burmeister & Wain engine would push her along at 15 knots. In 1985 she became the **Esso Saint Petersburg** after transferring to Esso International Shipping (Bahamas) under the Liberian flag. Five years later she was flying the British flag for Esso Marine UK Ltd as **Esso Tyne**. The Esso prefix was changed to **Petro** in 1994. As the **Petro Tyne** she continued to serve Esso until 1999. She was broken up at Alang in late 1999, sailing to the breakers as **Pet Ty**.

(John Wiltshire)

F T Everard and Sons took delivery of the **Audacity** in November 1968 from Goole Shipbuilding and Repairing Co Ltd. She was 699grt and had a 5-cylinder Newbury diesel power unit. She was a useful size coastal tanker and had ten tanks all fitted with heating coils. After a mere four years service, she was fitted with a new Deutz diesel engine of 1380bhp. The **Audacity** was 238 feet in length and had a draught of just over 14 feet. We see her here at Swansea negotiating the passage into the Queen's Dock on 17 October 1969, bathed in the morning sunshine. She remained within the Everard group until 1990 when she became the **Hawk** sailing for Dole S.A. under the Liberian flag. Subsequent names were the **Antares**, **Phoenix 1**, **Phoenix** (all in 1991) and then **Athina in** 1996. She still sails in 2008 as the **Saturn II** under the Honduras flag, and owned by Seneca Maritime Co, of Monrovia.

(John Wiltshire)

The **Stolt Idun** was built by Eriksberg Mekaniske Verkstad AB, of Gothenburg, in 1954. She has an interesting past as she was built for Norwegian ship owner Leif Hoegh & Co as the **Hoegh Skean**. She was sold in 1965 to I/S Saga Surf, of Oslo, becoming the **Saga Surf**. In 1967 she passed to Liberian flag owners who named her **Aktis** and later renamed her **Stolt Prince** for charter to Stolt Tankers. She then passed to Pam Shipping Ltd, of Monrovia, who named her **Pam** and then **Stolt Idun** in 1973. Seen from the beach below Penarth Head on 26 June 1976, the immaculate **Stolt Idun** has just sailed from Cardiff. When photographed, she flew the Greek flag and was registered in Piraeus. She is a motor tanker of 11582grt and has a 9-cylinder Burmeister and Wain oil engine of 7290bhp. Unfortunately this very smart tanker was delivered to breakers at Kaohsiung just over a year later on 20 August 1977. She was then broken up by E Chang Iron & Steel Works Co. Ltd.

(Bob Allen)

As briefly mentioned on page 57, Shell ordered 52 tankers of approximately 12000grt in 1951. The *Hemifusus* was delivered to Shell Bermuda (Overseas) Ltd, and placed under the British flag. She was one of ten H Class ships built by Cammell Laird & Co (Shipbuilders & Engineers) Ltd, of Birkenhead, and given names beginning with "Hemi". She was completed in 1954 and was 12182grt. She had a pair of Cammell Laird built geared steam turbines with an output of 8250shp. In February 1958 the *Hemifusus* would be the first tanker to take a cargo of crude oil from Port Harcourt in Nigeria. She was loaded by a smaller tanker just outside Bonny Bar. During her career she would also be used to carry refined oils. Twelve years later on 7 March 1970, she is seen at Cardiff having received attention including much new paintwork in the Bute Drydock. She is about to sail and her boilers are making some impressive black smoke. The *Hemifusus* would proceed from Cardiff to Barry Roads to undertake engine trials and await orders. She was eventually declared redundant in early 1976, and sent for breaking up at Burriana near Valencia in Spain.

(Bob Allen)

The rust-streaked tanker **Point Lacre** is seen on 30 March 1973 arriving at Avonmouth. She is a Liberian flagged ship operating for the Naves Shipping Corporation and registered in Monrovia. She was launched in Sweden on 15 February 1958, by Uddevallavarvet A/B of Uddevalla, and was handed over two months later. The **Point Lacre** was a motor ship, of 12467grt. She had a tank capacity of 875,000 cubic feet spread over 30 tanks, and also had 43,000 cubic feet available for dry cargo. Her main engine consisted of a 9-cylinder Gotaverken diesel of 8450bhp running at 112rpm which gave her a speed of 15 knots. In 1973 she was sold to Italian owner Morfini S.p.A., of Bari but quickly passed to Navisud S.p.A., also of Bari and was renamed the **Egnazia** under the Italian flag. As the **Egnazia** she was broken up in Italy at La Spezia in 1982.

(John Wiltshire)

The coastal tanker has always played an important role and we shall now look at some classic examples. The **Esso Preston** was a purpose-built bitumen carrier employed in Esso's UK coastal fleet. She was completed in March 1956 by Hall, Russell, of Aberdeen, and named after the Lancashire port that she often visited. The **Esso Preston** had a triple expansion engine of 1300ihp and she could carry 2050 tons of bitumen in her five cargo tanks. Each tank was kept at a temperature of between $280^{o}F$ and $300^{o}F$ by steam coils and her hull comprised two skins to help reduce heat loss. She could also be used to carry heavy fuel oil and was employed for a time supplying oil to Barking power station on the Thames. During her career she was involved in a collision at Grays in January 1963. She had a new starboard boiler fitted in 1972 (made in 1958). On 31 January 1975 she ran aground on the Cow and Calf rocks near Roches Point, County Cork. She was badly damaged being holed in three of her cargo spaces. She sailed to Cardiff a few days later and was examined in drydock. She was laid up at Cardiff until 27 March when she was towed away to Aviles to be scrapped by Spanish shipbreakers. Here she is seen being towed away from Cardiff on her final voyage to Spain.

(John Wiltshire)

The small coastal tanker **Blakeley** is seen approaching the south coast port of Shoreham on 15 August 1979. She was built in North Devon by Appledore Shipbuilders Ltd for Bowker and King Ltd of London. The date of her launch was 23 October 1971, and she was completed the following month. The **Blakeley** followed an identical vessel the **Bude**, completed at the same yard a month earlier. Bowker and King specialised in operating a fleet of coastal tankers around the UK coast which were often used to supply bunkers to ships in port. Other duties would include supplying refined products to smaller storage depots. Her dimensions were 211 feet overall length and 30 feet in the beam. She had a gross tonnage of 728. Her 800bhp Lister Blackstone engine pushed her along at 10 knots. She was sold in 1990 and became the **Rapide 1** for a Belgian owner. In 2001 she became the **Slops 8** working at Ambiliki in Greece. As the **Slops 8** she is believed still to be in service in 2008.

(Bernard McCall)

The **Wheeldale H.** was one of a number of similar self propelled tank barges constructed for John Harker Ltd. They were built on the River Aire at Harker's own yard at Knottingley from which she was launched broadside on 8 October 1953. The **Wheeldale H.** was yard number 254. She was 273grt and her hull was 135 feet in length by 21 feet 9 inches in the beam. Propulsion was by means of a 5-cylinder Blackstone diesel of 225bhp. Harker's vessels were to be seen all around the coast of the British Isles and some were based in the Bristol Channel. They were usually to be found transporting fuel from port installations to smaller depots often inland on canals and rivers. The **Wheeldale H.** is seen arriving at Barry in July 1970. She was sold for use in Nigeria by 1993, and is still believed to be active in 2007. In the background can be seen a cargo ship of the Saguenay Line which has just sailed from Barry.

(Andrew Wiltshire collection)

The coastal tanker **Shell Driller** started life as the **Empire Tedilla** being launched on 25 September 1945 for the Minsitry of War Transport. She was completed in early 1946 and entered service managed by the Anglo-Saxon Petroleum Company, gaining the name **Forskalia** in 1947. She was built by Laing at their Deptford yard in Sunderland and was 947grt and had an overall length of 193 feet. In 1949 she passed to J Harker, of Knottingley. as **Danesdale H.** before becoming the **Shell Driller** in 1952 for Shell Mex and BP Ltd. She was a motor tanker, her main engine with an output of 640bhp, being supplied by British Polar Engines Ltd, of Glasgow. Shell Mex and BP operated two other tankers that started life with the MoWT during in 1946. These were the **Shell Director** and **Shell Supplier**. At twenty years of age her days were to be over. The **Shell Driller** was broken up at Faslane after arriving there in August 1966. Here she is seen underway at Cork.

(Stan Tedford)

The Grangemouth Dockyard Co Ltd built the **Vacuum Pioneer** for the Vacuum Oil Company in 1953. She was the first tanker for their Coryton oil refinery being intended to operate initially between Coryton and Birkenhead. She was principally built as a bitumen carrier and had ten separate tanks with steam heating coils. Her gross tonnage was 1650grt. The **Vacuum Pioneer** also had provision to carry drums of grease in a small hold. Stephenson Clarke would remain her managers throughout her career. The **Vacuum Pioneer** had a triple expansion steam engine built by the North-Eastern Marine Engineering Co Ltd, of Sunderland, with an output of 1350ihp. She was a frequent visitor to the Bristol Channel. Here we see her leaving the Queen's Dock, Swansea, fully laden on 18 May 1970. Later the same year on 13 November, she was in collision with the Stephenson Clarke collier **Worthing** near Haisborough Sands. She was declared a total constructive loss and subsequently broken up at Blyth.

(John Wiltshire)

The unmistakable lines of the **Robert M** are clearly evident here. Having left the entrance of the Manchester Ship Canal at Eastham on 2 July 1983, she sails for Ardrossan fully laden. She is believed to have been the final example of a British coastal tanker with bridge situated amidships. She started life as the **Cree** and was delivered in January 1970 by the Hong Kong and Whampoa Dock Co Ltd of Hong Kong for Matheson & Co Ltd of London. She was built as a refined oil and bitumen carrier and has a gross tonnage of 1745grt. She was abandoned in position 11S 116E on 25 January 1974 after suffering an engine explosion and fire. She was eventually towed into Singapore and repaired. The **Cree** was then sold to Metcalf Motor Coasters Ltd, of Liverpool, in December 1976, and became **Robert M** in 1977. She has six cargo tanks all with heating coils, the bitumen being carried in the centre tanks. Her main engine is a 16-cylinder vee configuration diesel of 2200bhp built by M.A.N. in West Germany. She became the **Nesa 1** in 1997, and then **Nesa R.** later the same year, trading in the Persian Gulf.

(Roy Cressey)

The **Candourity** was one of five similar vessels purchased from the Admiralty by F T Everard and Sons Ltd in 1956 after a decade in service. All were built as coaling lighters by W J Yarwood and Sons Ltd, of Northwich, and had triple expansion engines. She was completed as **C641** on 28 March 1946. The other four gained the names **Conformity**, **Commodity**, **City** and **Clanity**. Between 1957 and 1960 they were rebuilt at Goole as coastal tankers, the **Candourity** being renamed in 1958. She was lengthened and widened to accommodate the insertion of a new tank section, and her gross tonnage changed from 352 to 474. The wheelhouse was located on the well deck with her masts and tall funnel being hinged, to allow access to up river oil berths on the River Thames. Her limited bunker capacity often restricted her duties, but during her service for Everard, she could be regularly found on the Thames and Medway. The **Candourity** was broken up by Van den Bosche & Co and arrived at Antwerp on 19 June 1969.

(John Wiltshire collection)

The **Ben Hittinger** was built in Bristol by Charles Hill and Sons for the National Benzole Company Limited. She was completed in July 1951 and was designed to carry petroleum products. In 1959 Shell-Mex and BP Ltd of London acquired the National Benzole business, and the **Ben Hittinger** joined this fleet. In 1961 she was lengthened from 160 feet to 181 feet which increased her gross tonnage from 446 to 522. The **Ben Hittinger** had a 6-cylinder British Polar diesel of 560bhp.

In 1972 she was sold to Ball & Plumb Shipping Co Ltd, of Gravesend, and became the **Spirit Carrier II**. In 1976 a further move saw her being purchased by J P Knight Ltd, of Rochester, and converted into a barge. For this role she carried the name **Kingsthorpe**. She was eventually sold for scrap in 1986. The **Ben Hittinger** is seen arriving at Swansea on 27 May 1970 to load a cargo.

(John Wiltshire)

Another well known UK operator of coastal tankers was C Rowbotham and Sons Ltd of London. This was a family company with its roots in Yorkshire. For many years their vessels were a frequent sight in the Bristol Channel. One such tanker is the **Guidesman** of 799grt which dated from 1964. She was launched by Drypool Engineering & Drydock Co Ltd, of Hull, on 16 September 1964. The **Guidesman** had ten cargo tanks and was powered by a 12-cylinder vee-type Brons 2-stroke diesel assembled by the shipbuilder. The **Guidesman** is seen here sailing from Avonmouth on 28 August 1970. She is wearing the older funnel markings which were phased out by Rowbotham in 1972. The **Guidesman** was sold in 1983 and passed to Greek owners Koutlakis & Leonardos as **Vasiliki IV**. She was later sold to other Greek owners in 1984. In 1987 she crossed the Atlantic and a new home in Venezuela, sailing as **Bianca Marie** for Maritima Canopus S.A. In November that year she suffered serious machinery damage. While being towed from Curaçao to Puerto Cabello, she was abandoned on an unknown beach.

(John Wiltshire)

We now look in more detail at the River Mersey and the Manchester Ship Canal which witnessed many splendid tankers over the years. The **El Lobo** was to be the final tanker to be delivered to the Lobitos Oilfields Ltd, of London. This was a small company whose vessels had for many years been managed by C T Bowring and Co Ltd. It would appear that when delivered in 1959, the **El Lobo** replaced the earlier tanker **El Gallo** of 1941. Lobitos Oilfields Ltd was originally founded in 1908 and eventually passed to the Burmah Oil Company in 1962. We see the **El Lobo** arriving at Eastham in the late afternoon of 18 July 1972, and in the colours of Burmah Oil Trading Ltd. She was a motor tanker of 12078grt and was launched on 22 December 1958. Her builder Swan, Hunter and Wigham Richardson, of Wallsend, installed a 6-cylinder Doxford opposed piston engine, built by the Wallsend Slipway & Engineering Co, which gave her a speed of 13 knots. During her days trading with Burmah Oil (she was still managed by Bowring), the **El Lobo** could be found at locations such as Curaçao, New York and Stanlow on the Manchester Ship Canal. The **El Lobo** carried the same name all her working life, and was broken up at Faslane in 1976.

(Paul Boot)

The **Caltex Kenya** was the first vessel in a series of four motor tankers from the Pallion yard of William Doxford & Sons Ltd in Sunderland. All four were built for Overseas Tankship (UK) Ltd for trading worldwide and in particular from Bahrein to India and east African ports. She was launched in September 1951 and completed in the following March. Her three sisterships followed in order as the **Caltex Tanganyika**, **Caltex Delhi** and **Caltex Calcutta**. The **Caltex Kenya** was 8523grt and had a 5-cylinder Doxford opposed piston type diesel engine of 5150bhp. She had 24 cargo tanks as well as a gastight cargo hold forward. Her hull was part welded and her self discharge rate was 1400 tons per hour using four pumps. Her three sisters were all sold for scrap between October 1966 and January 1967. The **Caltex Kenya** however went on to transfer to Texaco ownership and became the **Texaco Kenya** in 1968. In 1969 she passed to Texaco Panama without a change of name and was finally to arrive at Kaohsiung for breaking up on 30 October 1971. Here we see her at Runcorn on the Manchester Ship Canal. She is about the pass under the three bridges, including the old Runcorn Transporter Bridge which was still standing at the time.

(Eddie Jackson)

The **British Hazel** was the first vessel of an eleven ship series of products tankers, known as the "Tree" class, for the BP Tanker Co Ltd. She was built by Swan, Hunter and Wigham Richardson, at Wallsend, and launched on 31 October 1963. The class was constructed by six different yards including three in Sweden. Of 12964grt, she was powered by a 6-cylinder Sulzer engine assembled by Wallsend Slipway & Engineering Co. The **British Hazel** featured bridge control of her main engine. This incorporated a rapid and automated "ahead to astern" air-braking arrangement, and automatic recording of telegraph movements. She was designed to carry several grades of oil and was equipped with a complex arrangement of pumping machinery. The **British Hazel** was sold in 1982 to Petrostar Company Ltd, becoming **Petrostar XVII**. After several further changes of name she arrived at Alang in India to be broken up in January 2003. By this time she was carrying the name **Fal XVIII**.

(Eddie Jackson)

The **Overseas Adventurer** had an interesting and varied career. She was built in 1963 for London and Overseas Freighters Ltd by Rheinstahl Nordseewerke of Emden in West Germany. She was 13721grt and had 11 centre tanks and 22 wing tanks. Propulsion was from a 7-cylinder M.A.N. diesel of 8400bhp which gave her a sea speed of 14 knots. In 1973 the **Overseas Adventurer** was put on bareboat charter to the Ministry of Defence and allocated to the Royal Fleet Auxiliary as **Cherryleaf**. She performed this role until June 1980 when she reverted to her original name. In 1981 she was sold to the Petrostar Co Ltd of Saudi Arabia and became **Petrostar XVI**. On 5 April 1986 she became caught up in the Gulf Conflict and was hit by missiles fired by Iranian helicopters. She suffered casualties and was badly damaged. She was towed to Sharjah and eventually sold to Taiwan for scrap in early 1987. This photograph is dated 17 June 1971, and the rather shabby looking **Overseas Adventurer** is passing Seacombe, on her way down the Mersey.

(Paul Boot)

The **Damon** was a rather interesting motor tanker dating from 1955. She is seen here arriving at Eastham on the first day of 1971 in very low wintry sunshine. She was trading for Arab Shipping Corp S.A. and flying the Greek flag. She was launched on 22 April 1955 by Bartram & Sons Ltd, of South Dock, Sunderland, as the **George Lyras**. She was delivered to her owner Marine Enterprises Ltd (Lyras Brothers Ltd) the following September. On 7 April 1959 she went on long term charter to the Royal Fleet Auxiliary as a fleet replenishment tanker. She was renamed **Appleleaf**. Her gross tonnage was 11588 and she was 557 feet in length. Her main engine was a 6-cylinder Doxford of 6800bhp that was assembled at Wallsend by North-Eastern Marine Engineering Co Ltd. Her charter to the RFA ended in 1970 and she passed back to her owners who then sold her. The **Appleleaf** then became **Damon** under the Singapore flag. Ten years later in June 1980 she was sold to ship breakers at San Pedro in Argentina and was dismantled.

(Paul Boot)

Shell placed an order in 1951 for 52 steam-powered tankers of approximately 12000grt and 18000dwt. Six ships in this order were not however delivered to Shell. Within the Shell Group, the British vessels took names beginning with the letter H and those under the Dutch flag had names beginning with the letter K. The **Kalydon** was one of the latter. She was launched in October 1954 by the Rotterdamsche Dry Dock Maats and completed in February 1955. She was 12107grt and was built to carry both crude oil and refined products. Her 33 tanks were served by 4 cargo pumps with a capacity of 500 tons per hour. Accommodation was for 55 crew members. The Dutch flagged K class numbered only sixteen vessels, and four others (**Kabylia**, **Kara**, **Katelysia** and **Kelletia**) were built at the same yard as the **Kalydon**. All had turbine machinery assembled by the shipyard. The **Kalydon** seen here on 18 July 1975 in the Eastham Channel, and was broken up at Castellon in Spain during the summer of 1976.

(Paul Boot)

The classic pre-war motor tanker **Esso Plymouth** dates back to 1936, entering service as **Comanchee**. Built as Yard No 544, she was launched on 9 January 1936 by John Brown, Clydebank, for the Anglo-American Oil Co Ltd, Glasgow. She was 6837grt and 450 feet overall length by 61 feet in the beam. Her main machinery consisted of a 4-cylinder 2-stroke oil engine assembled by her builder. In 1950 her owners became restyled as the Esso Petroleum Company and the **Comanchee** became **Esso Plymouth**, still under the British flag. She was a regular caller to the Manchester Ship Canal where she is seen in this view towards the end of her career, berthed in the Runcorn lay-by. Her masts could be truncated to enable her to sail the full length of the canal. The tug/tender **Daniel Adamson** can be seen lying beyond her stern. The **Esso Plymouth** was eventually broken up at Grimstad in Norway, arriving there on 13 August 1962.

(Eddie Jackson)

The elderly tanker **Winamac**, seen arriving at Eastham, began life in 1939 as the **Mobilube** for the Socony-Vacuum Oil Co Inc, of New York. She was built by Bethlehem Steel Co Shipbuilding Division of Sparrows Point. She was launched on 29 April 1939 and would have an interesting career. On 19 January 1943 she was torpedoed by a Japanese submarine. Her machinery was badly damaged and she was considered a total loss. She did not sink, however, and was taken over by the US Navy for use as a storage vessel and renamed **YO-164**. In 1947 she passed back to her original owner Socony-Vacuum and was repaired. Her original machinery appears to have been retained, but in 1951 was replaced by a pair of steam turbines of 1946 vintage. In 1954 she became the **Winamac** for the Brilliant Transportation Co S.A. under the Panamanian flag. In 1957 she passed to Mobil Tankers Co S.A. of Panama and was extensively rebuilt. She was lengthened from 488 feet to 525 feet, widened and deepened with new cargo tanks. Her gross tonnage rose from 10222 to 11981. She passed to Iberian Tankers Co in 1963 still sailing as **Winamac** under the Panamanian flag. She continued to do so until 1972, her final voyage was to Taiwan in December of that year. Here she was dismantled on the beaches of Kaohsiung in early 1973.

(Eddie Jackson)

The T2 was an American tanker design, built in World War 2 and made available for commercial use after hostilities ended. We shall look at some examples on the next four pages. The original design was T2-A and was developed to include the T2-SE-A1 and T2-SE-A2. In principle the **Conoco Humber** was a T2-SE-A1, but was in fact three ships rebuilt into one. She was completed in October 1945 as the **Atlantic Ranger** for Atlantic Refining of Philadelphia. She was 10602grt and 16613dwt. Her builder was Sun Shipbuilding and Drydock Co, of Chester, Pennsylvania, and her propulsion followed others of this type being a turbo-electric power plant and single screw. She changed ownership in 1954 moving to the Liberian flag and again in 1963 when she gained the new name **Angela**. In 1964 she passed to the Seacrest Investment Co, of Monrovia, and was drastically

rebuilt. Her forepart was scrapped and her aft section was mated with the forepart of the tanker **Waneta** to produce a 17563grt vessel. The new vessel was 597 feet in length and gained the name **Santa Suzana**. In 1967 the fore section of the **Santa Suzana** was removed for use elsewhere. The aft section was then joined to the forepart of the **Ponca City** to form a ship 523 feet in length. This was given the name **Suzana S**. In this final guise the ship continued to sail for Seacrest until 1967, when she became the **Conoco Humber** of World Wide Transport Inc, Monrovia. She visited Cardiff to discharge refined products and is seen here on 5 April 1969 with just a few months still to trade. Just two years after her final surgery she was scrapped at La Spezia arriving there 14 July 1969.

(John Wiltshire)

The original T2 tanker design was based on a pair of American-built tankers, the **Mobilfuel** and **Mobilube** of 1939 (see page 59). The **Haravgi** was a larger T2 type tanker of the T2-SE-A2 variety, and was built for the US War Shipping Administration in 1944 as the **Mission Santa Maria**. She came from the Sausalito yard of Marinship Corporation and was launched on 4 July 1944. Her original grt was given as 10470 and her principal dimensions were an overall length of 523 feet with a beam of 68 feet. She was sold into commercial operation in 1948 as the Panamanian flag **Cyrus**. She became the **John** in 1950 and was lengthened to 545 feet in 1951. Her gross tonnage became 11625grt. She underwent a further five name changes from 1953, passing through the hands of Greek, Liberian and Argentine owners until becoming **Haravgi** in 1966. She was now under the Greek flag again and sailing for John S Latsis, of Athens and London. She is seen at Cardiff on 31 May 1968. In 1969 she became the **Galeta** of Galeta Ocean Equipment & Shipping Co, Panama, and was converted to an offshore oil supply ship in 1970. Her final days were as the **Sept Iles**, from 1971 until she was scrapped at Split in the former Yugoslavia in 1973.

(John Wiltshire)

The **Texaco Bombay** was built in 1945 as the **Castle's Wood** at Chester, Pennsylvania, for the War Shipping Administration in the United States. Her builder Sun Shipbuilding and Drydock Co was heavily involved in the construction of T2 tankers for the Emergency Tanker Building Programme. The **Castle's Wood** was of the T2-SE-A1 type, of which 481 were built between 1942 and 1945. By 1951 she had become the **Caltex Bombay** under the British flag and ownership of Overseas Tankship (UK) Ltd. In 1968 she was subjected to major surgery. She was lengthened, widened and deepened. Her gross tonnage rose from 10691 to 13892. She was now 575 feet in length compared to 524 feet when built. Her amidships accommodation was moved aft, and a new tall funnel added in place of the original stack. Also at this time, she was renamed **Texaco Bombay**, to reflect the new style name of her owner Texaco. Her machinery remained unaltered. She was powered by Westinghouse turbo-electric propulsion of 7240shp. Time was eventually called in August 1982 when she arrived at Kaohsiung in Taiwan. She would be run up onto a beach in a controlled operation so that scrapping could commence. We see her in the oil dock at Avonmouth on 8 August 1976. Her original profile would have been similar to that of the vessel on page 60.

(John Wiltshire)

The tanker **Concho** was also the result of a major rebuild. In fact only the aft section containing her machinery remained of the original ship. This section was built by Kaiser Co Inc of Portland, Oregon, and started life in 1945 as the **Bradford Island**, a T2 type tanker of the T2-SE-A1 variety. T2 tankers tended to be named after monuments, national parks, forts, lakes, battles etc. The **Bradford Island** was sold for commercial operation in 1948. The fore and cargo sections were built in 1970 by the Bethlehem Steel Corporation of Beamont, Texas. She became **Concho** in 1979. Her steam turbine developed 7240shp which drove a single generator of 5400kw. This supplied power to a single General Electric propulsion motor. She was oil-fired and in her final form could achieve 13 knots. On 19 January 1981 the **Concho** suffered structural damage at Kill van Kull and was deliberately grounded in Gravesend Bay near Brooklyn. Unfortunately 500,000 gallons of oil were spilt into the local waters. She is seen here near Corpus Christi on 17 September 1996 in the colours of her owners, Sabine Towing and Transportation of Houston, Texas. Her years with Sabine were spent US coasting to ports such as Los Angeles, Pascagoula and New York. She passed to Hvide Marine Inc, of Fort Lauderdale, in 1998 and became **HMI Trader**. She was sold to Indian ship breakers in 2000, and she arrived at Alang on 28 August for dismantling.

(Nigel Jones)

Our next section reviews tankers owned in various countries of north-west Europe. France, West Germany, Belgium and the Netherlands had sizeable fleets of tankers sailing worldwide. The Dutch flag **Ameland** was one of the six tankers that Shell ordered in 1951 but did not take delivery of (see page 57). Three were delivered to UK flag owners, and the other three to Dutch fleets. The **Ameland** was the first of the trio delivered to Dutch owners. She was in fact launched in August 1956 as the **Kraussina** for Shell, but completed as **Ameland** for the Rotterdam Steamship Co. She was built by P Smit Jr, of Rotterdam, and was 12159grt and 18527dwt. She transferred to Holland Bulk Transport in 1970, hence the letters HBT on her funnel. She was eventually broken up at Bilbao after arrival there in April 1976. The **Ameland** was photographed around mid-day on 4 February 1972 having just sailed from Eastham, and making some fine black smoke. Beyond her grey hull and unfamiliar funnel markings, the classic lines of the K class Shell tanker become apparent.

(Paul Boot)

The French flagged tanker **President André Blanchard** was built in 1955 by J Boel & Fils, Tamise, Belgium, as the **Betty Maersk**. She was 8754grt and 479 feet in length. She was built for Danish ship-owner A P Møller Ltd, and was the last vessel in a series of five similar ships. Møller operated a large fleet of both steam and motor tankers at this time. In 1963 she passed to Société Nationale des Petroles d'Aquitaine and given the new name **Lacq III**. The following year she was rebuilt to carry chemicals as well as oil for the same owner. Her gross tonnage changed to 8715grt and she was renamed **President André Blanchard**. With Bayonne as her port of registry she is seen here sailing along the New Waterway on 19 May 1972. Her lines are not really enhanced by her cluttered deck areas. The end was to come for this ship in October 1977 when she arrived at San Esteban de Pravia in Spain to be broken up.

(Paul Boot)

The **Belgulf Progress** was a Belgian flagged steam tanker that entered service in 1959 for Belgulf Tankers S.A. Together with her sistership **Belgulf Glory**, also of 1959, she was a regular visitor to British waters employed in the transport of refined oil products. She was built by Furness Shipbuilding Co Ltd at Haverton Hill on the River Tees and was 556 feet in length with a gross tonnage of 12018grt. She had a pair of steam turbines built by Richardsons Westgarth (Hartlepool) Ltd with an output of 8200shp. Steam was supplied by a pair of water-tube oil-fired boilers. The **Belgulf Progress** was sold in 1975 and became **United Progress** of Hamilton Bay Shipping Co Ltd, of Monrovia. Her fate was realised when she arrived at Kaohsiung for breaking up on 29 July 1977. She had been purchased by Yung Tai Steel and Iron Works Co Ltd and work commenced on 5 September. This view was dated 24 February 1973 when the **Belgulf Progress** was seen arriving at Eastham.

(Paul Boot)

The **Diala** was a German flagged Shell tanker, and is seen passing beneath Tancarville Bridge on the River Seine, outward bound from Rouen on 21 July 1985. She was launched in April 1966 by Deutsche Werft A/G of Hamburg for Deutsche Shell Tanker GmbH. She was one of three similar crude oil tankers built at this yard for Shell. The other pair, **Darina** and **Drupa**, sailed under the British flag. A fourth vessel the **Dolabella** was built at St. Nazaire for Shell's French fleet. All had distinctive twin funnels. In addition to these four steam tankers no less than 14 motor tankers of similar size were constructed at around the same period, 1966/67. The gross tonnage of the **Diala** was 39426grt and she was just under

800 feet in length. She had a pair of Stal-Laval steam turbines developing 16000shp and a normal service speed of 15.5 knots. In 1988 she became **Lan Shui** and sailed for Cincia Shipping Corporation under the Liberian flag. The same year she was converted into a floating production storage vessel and by 1989 was based in the Intan Oilfield of Indonesia. In January 1990 she suffered a serious engine room fire and was placed in lay-up at Brunei in 1991. In late 1992 she was converted into a storage unit by Sembawang Shipyard. Her damaged aft section was removed and towed away to China where it was scrapped by October 1993.

(Bernard McCall)

We now look at some tankers out of work and laid up in the River Fal on the south coast of Cornwall. For many years this been a popular sheltered, deep water location to lay up shipping of all types. Tankers were to be found here in abundance in the 1970s and 1980s. Two vessels of Purfina-Transports are seen moored together on 3 September 1975 near the King Harry Ferry. Nearest the camera is the *Fina America* with the similar *Fina Angola* (1959/21851grt) moored alongside her. The *Fina America* was built in 1958 and was 21401grt (35941dwt). The origin of Purfina can be traced back to 1923, when Belgian oil refiner PetroFina (established in 1920) was anxious to set up a company to market its products in western Europe. Purfina was jointly established with American Pure Oil Company and had ships under French, Italian, Dutch and Belgian flags. The *Fina America* was the only one of five similar ships that was placed under the Belgian flag. She was a steam tanker built by Ch. Nav. de La Ciotat in southern France. She was to trade again after leaving the River Fal as she became the *Deepwater Bay* in 1976. This was to be short lived as on 19 November 1977 she suffered an explosion and fire whilst at Luanda. She was subsequently towed away to be scrapped in Taiwan in April 1978.

(John Wiltshire)

The world's first purpose-built commercial methane tankers entered service in 1964. One was named **Methane Princess** and was designed to carry liquefied natural gas from Arzew in Algeria to a terminal at Canvey Island in the Thames Estuary. This was claimed to be a 12-day round trip. She was owned by Conch Methane Tankers Ltd and managed by Shell Tankers (UK) Ltd. She was built by Vickers-Armstrong (S.B.) Ltd at Barrow-in-Furness. She was 21876grt and 24608dwt and was fitted with a fully automated cargo data recording system. The **Methane Princess** was propelled by a pair of Vickers Pametrada type steam turbines of 13750shp. Steam was supplied by two Foster Wheeler water tube boilers and she had a speed in excess of 17 knots. Her liquefied cargo was stored at -162.2°C in nine specially constructed tanks. Each tank was built from aluminium and insulated with balsa panels augmented by glass fibre. With a cargo of this nature, "boil off" occurs at the alarming rate of 0.3% per day. However, on the **Methane Princess** this was collected by pumps and consumed by the ships boilers which had special gas/oil fuel burners. The **Methane Princess** is seen laid up on the River Fal on 9 August 1982 with her sistership **Methane Progress** alongside. The **Methane Progress** was sold for scrap in 1986 after five years in lay up. The **Methane Princess** though was pressed back into service. She survived until 1997, when she was broken up at Alang in India.

(John Wiltshire)

Another tanker dating from the 1950s and laid up out of work was the Liberian flag **Neso**. Unusually for a Scandinavian tanker of this era she was the product of a Japanese shipyard. The **Neso** was laid down on 1 August 1956 as the **Rosborg** and launched on 20 February 1957 by Hitachi Shipbuilding & Engineering Co Ltd at its Sakurajima Shipyard in Osaka. She was delivered to Danish owner A/S D/S Dannebrog (C K Hansen managers) and was 12410grt. She passed to Borgships, of Monrovia, in 1965 and became the **Rosy** in 1968 for Ina Tanker Corporation, of Lugano but continuing to sail under the Liberian flag. She then became the **Serena** in 1973 for Serena Shipping Co Ltd who renamed her **Neso** in 1974. As the **Neso** she is seen here on 3 September 1975 with the French flagged tanker **Olympie** of 1958 lying alongside her. After being laid up on the Fal since 18 March 1975, the **Neso** was sold to Spanish breakers and towed away from Falmouth on 11 April 1976 by the Spanish tug **Faneca**. During stormy weather the tow broke and the **Neso** went aground near Aviles on 15 April. She was scrapped at this location, demolition commencing on 1 June 1976.

(John Wiltshire)

Over the next five pages we will be taking a look at some tankers with special roles. The first of three similar Royal Fleet Auxiliary tankers was ordered in February 1963 and was to be named **Olynthus**. She was delivered from Hawthorn, Leslie (S.B.) Ltd, Newcastle in June 1965 as a fleet replenishment vessel, providing fuel and extensive stores. She had a crew of 88 RFA personnel, and being a military vessel was fitted for armaments and had provision for three helicopters. She was built to a high specification with air conditioning and automation of her machinery space. Her turbines could be accurately controlled from her bridge, which aided "station keeping" whilst refuelling other ships at sea.

Because of confusion of her name with that of the **Olympus**, she was renamed **Olwen** in August 1967, by which time she carried pennant number A122. Her pair of 26500shp turbines gave her a maximum speed of 21 knots. She was laid up at Portsmouth in 1999 and renamed **Kea** in May 2001, before being towed away to ship breakers at Aliaga. She did not, however, succumb to the Turkish breakers, and was resold to Indian breakers. She was beached at Alang on 31 July 2001. We see the **Olwen** at anchor in Plymouth Sound on 16 August 1997.

(Nigel Jones)

Palm Line Ltd, of London, operated the purpose-built vegetable oil carrier **Matadi Palm** which was completed in December 1970. She was their last tanker and replaced the older vessel **Makurdi Palm** of 1953. She was built to trade between west Africa and north west Europe with cargoes such as unrefined coconut oil, groundnut oil and palm oil. In the opposite direction she would carry refined rapeseed oil. The **Matadi Palm** was built by Swan Hunter Shipbuilders Ltd at Haverton Hill and was 8870grt. The **Matadi Palm** apparently suffered from a major design flaw. She was constructed with no double bottom tanks. Her 28 main cargo

tanks had steam coils designed to keep her expensive cargo at 96ºF. During winter in northern Europe however, this was not sufficient to heat the oil at the bottom of her hull. Recovery of this oil was not straight forward and was also very time consuming. The **Matadi Palm** was taken over by United African Conference International Ltd in 1985 and her name was shortened to **Matadi**. She ended her days in 1995 as the **Lian** on the Indian ship-breaking beaches at Alang. Here she passes along the New Waterway on 28 May 1975.

(Nigel Jones)

The *Platidia*, seen here at Cardiff on 10 May 1972, has just been undocked from the Bute Drydock. Together with her sistership *Plagiola* she was built as a bitumen carrier for La Corona N.V. Petroleum Mij. (part of the Royal Dutch Shell group of companies). When new they were destined to work out of Curaçao and Aruba trading to the east coast of the USA. The *Platidia* dates from 1955 and is 11007grt (15342dwt). She was launched at the Hamburg yard of Deutsche Werft A/G on 3 November 1954 and completed in the following March. For the carriage of bitumen she had ten centre tanks that were wider than normal and which were fitted with large capacity conical steam heating coils. The narrower wing tanks were used only for ballast. The cargo pumps for bitumen discharge were of the reciprocating type as opposed to turbine driven pumps found on Shell's H, K and A class tankers. Both *Platidia* and *Plagiola* were steam tankers with machinery built by German turbine builder AEG. The *Platidia* was 525 feet in length and was capable of 14 knots. She was broken up at Castellon in Spain in early 1974.

(John Wiltshire)

The Italian flagged liquefied gas tanker **Enrico Fermi** is seen arriving at Swansea on 10 March 1988. She will be loading a cargo of locally produced liquefied petroleum gas. Her three cargo tanks held 7500 cubic metres of LPG. The **Enrico Fermi** was named after the physicist who built the first experimental nuclear reactor. She had quite distinctive lines and was the product of Cant. Nav. M. & B. Benetti's yard at Viareggio near Livorno in Tuscany. She was built in 1977 and had a gross tonnage of 5394grt. Main power was from a pair of Fiat 6-cylinder medium speed diesels, geared to a single propeller shaft. In this view she is operating for Carbofin SpA and registered in Palermo. The **Enrico Fermi** became the **Pauline** in 1994 for Isomarine S.A. under the Panamanian flag. Her final guise from 1997 was as the **Astoria**, owned Miramar Gas Corp, also Panamanian flag. As the latter she arrived at Mumbai in India on 5 March 2003 to be broken up.

(Bob Allen)

The unmistakeable orange colour scheme tells us that the **Bow Rogn** is a chemical tanker. She flies the Norwegian flag and is owned by S/A Storli of Bergen and managed by A/S Rederiet Odfjell. The **Bow Rogn** was built in 1970 by Moss Vaerft & Dokk A/S of Moss and was 6673grt and 10033dwt. Her hull was 396 feet in length and was ice strengthened. Her cargo tanks consisted of two conventional tanks and fifteen stainless steel tanks for carrying chemicals. Her main engine was an Akers/Nylands built Burmeister & Wain of 5400bhp, driving a controllable pitch propeller. In 1980 she was sold and became the **Jo Rogn** for S/A Hassel, with J O Odfjell as managers. In 1983 she was renamed **Betula** under the Norwegian flag. She met an unfortunate end as on 28/29 June 1993, she was wrecked north of Lazaro Cardenas in Mexico. In happier times we see her as **Bow Rogn** visiting the South Wales port of Barry to discharge chemicals on 17 November 1972.

(John Wiltshire)

Our next section takes us to the River Tyne which was the birthplace of many tankers and would also be refuge for many returning to be repaired. For many years, tracing right back to the **British Aviator** of 1924, the British Tanker Co Ltd and its predecessors favoured motor ships. Despite this, here we have a steam-powered tanker. Completed in March 1958 for the BP Tanker Co Ltd, the **British Faith** was in its day regarded as a "super-tanker". She was one of a series of eight vessels based on an earlier series of six ships, and was registered to the subsidiary Tanker Charter Co Ltd. Along with the **British Glory** she was built by Vickers-Armstrong Ltd at Barrow as a 31981dwt crude oil carrier with 30 cargo tanks. Her main machinery consisted of a pair of steam turbines of 15500shp

assembled by Vickers-Armstong (Engineering) Ltd and could achieve 15 knots. All eight vessels in this class were sold in 1973. The **British Faith** passed to Wonco Comp. Nav. S.A. as **Stelios** under the Greek flag. In 1976 she became **Montaza** retaining her Greek registry, but by October of that year she had arrived at Kaohsiung for breaking up. Here we see her at the Tyne Tanker Cleaning Company berth at North Shields on 30 June 1968. This facility was used to clear slops and ventilate the cargo tanks, thus allowing the issue of a gas-free certificate for hot work to be carried out. The ship would then move to one of the repair yards on the river.

(Bernard Kent)

Photographed in Brigham and Cowan's drydock at South Shields in September 1966 is the **Border Minstrel**. She was one of a series of ten similar vessels built for the Lowland Tanker Company Ltd, of Newcastle. These included the first in the series, the **Border Regiment** of 1953, and the final example delivered, the **Border Terrier** of 1956. The **Border Minstrel** was launched in August 1954 and completed later that year on 15 December by Blythswood Shipbuilding Company, of Scotstoun. She was a motor tanker with a 7040bhp 6-cylinder Doxford oil engine built by David Rowan and Co, Glasgow. Her dimensions were 547 feet in length by 69 feet in the beam, with a gross tonnage of 11389grt. The Lowland Tanker ships had a red funnel with black top separated by a tartan band bearing the BP Shield. Also visible in this view on the opposite side of the river are the Liberian flagged bauxite carrier **Discoverer**, and in one of the drydocks is Booker Line's **Booker Venture** being lengthened. The **Border Minstrel** was broken up at Bilbao in northern Spain in 1972. In 1976 BP took over the management of the remaining vessels and bought the outstanding shares in 1979.

(Bernard Kent)

On 10 June 1964 a lot of interest would have been centred around the Wallsend yard of Swan, Hunter and Wigham Richardson. It was on this day that the steam tanker **Ottawa** was launched. She would hold two records at that time. The **Ottawa** was the largest tanker to be placed under the British flag, and the largest ship to be built in the north-east of England. She was 51994grt (93231dwt) and was built for Trident Tankers Ltd, of London. This was the newly-formed company set up to manage all the P & O Group's tankers. She was 851 feet overall length and 125 feet in the beam. She was powered by a pair of geared steam turbines of 27100shp, manufactured by Wallsend Slipway and Engineering Co. The **Ottawa** ceased trading as a tanker in 1978 when ownership was transferred to Sea Transport Services Ltd. She was rebuilt at Singapore as a Moored Oil Storage Barge and placed on bareboat charter to Conoco Inc. Under the new name of **Udang Natuna** she was placed under the Liberian flag and allocated to the Udang oilfield in Indonesia. As the **Udang Natuna** she was eventually broken up at Alang in 1991.

(Malcolm Donnelly)

Seen on 5 May 1962 at Dunston-on-Tyne is the small steam tanker *Gadinia*, her days over. She is to be broken up here by Clayton and Davie. She was built for N.V. Curaçaosche Scheeps Maats by Smith's Dock Co Ltd at Middlesbrough in 1950. She is another tanker to have had an interesting and specialised role in her early years. The *Gadinia* was one of more than 12 similar twin-screw, shallow draught tankers built especially for service on Lake Maracaibo, Venezuela, in the post-war years. Following the discovery of oil by Shell under the lake in 1914 a navigational hazard obstructed its removal by sea. This hazard was a sand bar located at the entrance to the lake from the Caribbean, which restricted the draught of ships to thirteen feet. As there was no local market for the oil on the shores of Lake Maracaibo, it was initially towed away in tank barges to an oil refinery 50 miles off the Venezuelan coast at Willemstad, Curaçao. A special fleet of tankers was later built to ship oil from the lake, and became known as the "mosquito fleet". The *Gadinia* passed to Compania Shell de Venezuela Ltd, Maracaibo, in 1953. She continued her original role until 1961 when she passed to Shell Tankers (UK) Ltd, and returned to Europe. The *Gadinia* was 5924grt and was powered by two reciprocating steam engines.

(Malcolm Donnelly)

The distinctive funnel markings consisting of a blue seven pointed star over white and red bands gives us a clue that the **Teesfield** was associated with Hunting and Sons Ltd of North Shields. In fact the **Teesfield** was built for their subsidiary company Hunting (Eden) Tankers Ltd. She was completed by the Furness Shipbuilding Co Ltd at its Haverton Hill yard on Teesside in August 1959, having been launched in the previous February. She was a fairly conventional motor tanker of 12146grt and 18025dwt. Her main engine was a 6-cylinder diesel of 6600bhp to a Doxford opposed-piston design, and built by the Wallsend Slipway and Engineering Co. This 2-stroke engine was capable of running on heavy fuel oil. The **Teesfield** only ever traded for Hunting, and did so until 1978 when she arrived at Inverkeithing in the Firth of Forth for breaking up. Here we see her arriving on the Tyne on 3 April 1961.

(Malcolm Donnelly)

During the late 1960s tankers continued to grow in size. One reason for this was the need to meet the demand for oil in northern Europe. The steam tanker **Texaco Westminster** entered service in 1968 for Texaco Overseas Tankships and was registered in London. She was laid down as **Regent Westminster** at Swan, Hunter & Tyne (Shipbuilders) Ltd, Wallsend, and entered service as **Texaco Westminster** in June 1968. She was photographed being moved along the Tyne on 17 June 1968. Her main duty was to transport crude oil from the Persian Gulf to Europe. At 102602dwt, she was the first vessel in the Texaco fleet to exceed 100,000dwt. Her hull was 837 feet overall length and 127 feet breadth. In 1977, whilst receiving attention in a floating drydock at Palermo in Sicily, a storm struck the area, driving the drydock and tanker on to the shore. The ship was damaged and repaired at Genoa and later in Greece. The **Texaco Westminster** became a victim of the world surplus of supertankers that occurred in the mid to late 1970s. After only ten years service she was declared redundant and broken up at Kaohsiung in Taiwan in late 1978.

(Malcolm Donnelly)

Left : Often the most distinguishing features of a ship was its funnel marking. The Hadley Shipping Co had a very distinctive funnel marking and is seen here to very good effect on their tanker **Cerinthus** (see page 1). The **Cerinthus** was the third vessel in the Hadley fleet to carry this name. She was intended as a crude oil carrier and spent much of her time trading along the east coast of the USA, the Caribbean and South America. Her final commercial voyage was from Swansea to Stanlow refinery on Merseyside, and then the one-way trip to the scrap yard.

Right : The funnel shown here is that of the **Conoco Jet**, she was a Japanese-built motor tanker dating from 1956 and of 12807grt. She was built as **Merchantile Trader** by Uraga Dock, of Yokosuka. In this view she flies the Liberian flag and carries the funnel colours of World Wide Transport Inc. She was broken up at Chittagong in 1984, and is seen here at Cardiff on a bright November morning in 1969.

Below : The **British Resource** is seen here at Swansea in June 1969 wearing the old funnel colours of the BP Tanker Co Ltd. This was changed in 1968, together with the houseflag, to the colours shown on the **British Patrol** (see page 40). At this time the hull colour also changed from dark grey to black.

(all John Wiltshire)